Anson D. F. Randolph

Easter chimes

Anson D. F. Randolph

Easter chimes

ISBN/EAN: 9783741196249

Manufactured in Europe, USA, Canada, Australia, Japa

Cover: Foto ©Lupo / pixelio.de

Manufactured and distributed by brebook publishing software (www.brebook.com)

Anson D. F. Randolph

Easter chimes

Anne S. Paton
 from her friend
 A. D. F. Randolph,
April 15,
 1881.

"Arise, shine; for thy light is come, and the glory of the Lord is risen upon thee." Isa. lx. 1.

Arise, for He is risen to-day!
   And shine, for He is glorified!
Put on thy beautiful array,
   And keep perpetual Easter-tide.

EASTER CHIMES.

Oh, mountain height, break forth and sing
 In color music fair and sweet!
Oh, forest depths, awake and bring
 Your delicate odors to His feet!
  Sing, for the Lord hath done it!
  Proclaim redemption, for He won it!
Let Easter hallelujahs rise from every living
   thing!

NEW YORK:
ANSON D. F. RANDOLPH & COMPANY,
900 BROADWAY, COR. 20th ST.

COPYRIGHT, 1881, BY
ANSON D. F. RANDOLPH & COMPANY.

EDWARD O. JENKINS,   ROBERT RUTTER,
Printer and Stereotyper.   *Binder.*

It is too calm to be a dream,
Too gravely sweet, too full of power,
Prayer changed to praise this very hour!
　Yes, heard and answered! though it seem
Beyond the hope of yesterday,
Beyond the faith that dared to pray,
Yet not beyond the love that heard,
And not beyond the faithful word
On which each trembling prayer may rest
And win the answer truly best.

　Yes, heard and answered! sought and found!
I breathe a golden atmosphere
Of solemn joy, and seem to hear
　Within, above, and all around,
The chime of deep cathedral bells,
An early herald peal that tells
A glorious Easter-tide begun;
While yet are sparkling in the sun
Large raindrops of the night storm passed,
And days of Lent are gone at last.

FRANCES RIDLEY HAVERGAL.

CONTENTS.

	PAGE
Bright Easter Skies,	9
"Ring, Ring, O Easter Bells!"	12
Easter Morning,	15
New Hope,	17
"Oh, Lightly Part, Ye Purple Clouds,"	19
The Merry Church Bells,	22
"Hallelujah, Raise the Song,"	24
A Carol,	26
The Lord is Risen Indeed!	29
The Resurrection Light,	31
"Out of the Dust and the Darkness,"	33
"When Dawns on Earth the Easter Sun,"	36
At the Sepulchre,	39
Sweet Surprises,	41
"This Same Jesus,"	43
"O Comfort Ye my People!"	47

CONTENTS.

EASTER LESSONS,	50
AN EASTER SONG,	53
THE DEAR OLD STORY,	57
WOMAN'S EASTER,	59
THE CROCUS CROSS,	61
"EASTER LILIES, SWEET AND WHITE,"	63
THE EASTER GUEST,	65
GOD'S FLOWERS UPON GOD'S ALTAR,	67
"WAKE, MY CHILDREN!"	69
"SING, CHILDREN, SING!"	71
AN EASTER PRAYER,	74
MYRRH-BEARERS,	76
EASTER SUNDAY,	79
THE EASTER GREETING,	82
HE IS THY LIFE,	85
THE INESTIMABLE LOVE,	87
FOREVER WITH THE LORD,	91

BRIGHT EASTER SKIES.

BRIGHT Easter skies!
   Fair Easter skies!
Our Lord is risen:
We too shall rise.
Nor walls of stone, hewn firm and cold,
Nor Roman soldiers brave and bold,
Nor Satan's marshalled hosts could keep
The piercèd hands in deathly sleep;
Just as the Easter day-beams dawn,
Our buried Lord is risen and gone!

   Loud Easter bells!
   Rich Easter bells!
   A ransomed world
   Your chiming tells.
Let hills and rocks your gladness peal!
Behold the stone and broken seal!

BRIGHT EASTER SKIES.

Angels in white from heaven's bright way,
The useless clothes together lay;
Then sit serene, at head and feet,
The earliest saints with joys to greet.

> Green Easter fields!
> Fair Easter fields!
> Heaven's first ripe fruit
> Death conquered yields.

In Church-yards wide the seeds we sow,
Beneath the Cross the wheat shall grow;
One Easter Day death's reign shall end,
And golden sheaves shall heavenward send.
Hail the blest morn, by whose glad light
Angels shall reap the harvest white!

> Sweet Easter flowers!
> White Easter flowers!
> From heaven descend
> Life-giving showers.

Each plant that bloomed at Eden's birth,
Shall blow again o'er ransomed earth.

BRIGHT EASTER SKIES.

Pluck lilies rare and roses sweet,
And strew the path of Jesus' feet;
Throw fragrant palms before our King,
And wreathe the crown the saved shall bring!

    O Christian child!
    O Christian men!
    Our Victor Lord
    Shall come again.
Wake we our hearts at His command;
Lift we our love to His right hand;
With warmest hopes, to Easter skies,
Stretch we our arms and fix our eyes:
Till in the clouds His sign we see,
And quick and dead shout Jubilee!   AMEN.

THE BISHOP OF QUINCY.

"RING, RING, O EASTER BELLS!"

RING, ring, O Easter Bells!
   Ring, for the rosy hills of dawn,
Shine 'neath the feet of Easter Morn!
   Ring till your long, clear, tidal swells
Flood the wide earth with silvern sound!
   Ring for the battle fought and won!
Ring for the Victor throned and crowned;
   For death destroyed and sin undone!

   Ring, ring, O Easter Bells!
Ring out the love that will not cease
To weep o'er brows where all is peace,
   Ring out black weeds and funeral knells;
Ring in the love that walks in light
   Of healing hope, and lifts its eyes
From lily wreaths to saints in white,
   From empty graves to Paradise!

"*RING, RING, O EASTER BELLS!*"

Ring, ring, O Easter Bells!
Ring cheerily and bravely, where
Bowed hearts the daily burden bear
   Of growing thirst 'mid failing wells;
Ring out the dread, the doubt, the gloom,
   That hover round on murmuring wings:
Ring in the faith whose teeming womb
   Is quick with hints of better Springs!

Ring, ring, O Easter Bells!
Ring out the wide, wild, bitter cry
Of hearts that break, and souls that die,
   In grimy streets and noisome cells:
Ring in white Charity, to trace
   Through soil and want the Master's tread,
And learn to know His blessèd face
   In washing feet and breaking bread!

Ring, ring, O Easter Bells!
Ring out the old man, born in sin;
The new man, born in Christ, ring in;
   Ring in the living-water wells!

14 "*RING, RING, O EASTER BELLS!*"

Ring in the Bridegroom and the Bride ;
   Ring in the one, true, great High-Priest ;
Ring in the pearly gates oped wide ;
   Ring in the endless Marriage Feast !
     Ring, ring, O Easter Bells !

W. M. L. JAY.

EASTER MORNING.

OVER the purple mountains
   The Easter morn breaks clear,
And the sunbeams come as brightly,
   With their voiceless faith and cheer,
As to the waiting women
   Came the light of that hallowed day,
After their night of watching
   At the tomb where the Saviour lay.

As sweetly and as freshly
   Our Easter blossoms bloom
As those in that sunny garden
   Beside the Saviour's tomb;
Teaching the same glad lessons :
   That life must upward spring,
That to our flowers immortal
   No taint of earth can cling.

EASTER MORNING.

Oh, risen, glorious Saviour,
    What have we now to-day?
What gift of love and service
    At Thy pierced feet to lay?
Only our contrite hearts,
    But we offer them to Thee,
Praying that Thou wilt plant therein
    Fair lilies of purity.

Thou hast robbed the grave of terror,
    No more we fear its power;
Death is no more a monarch
    Since Thy resurrection hour.
Oh, happy, holy Sabbath,
    That saw our Lord arise!
He waits to welcome His redeemed
    Beyond the starry skies.

H. E. W.

NEW HOPE.

COME in glory, sun of Easter,
    And triumphant mount the skies,
For this day to bliss eternal
    Jesus from the grave did rise.

Since o'er hill and valley sounded
    The creative " Let there be,"
Earth ne'er knew, O holy morning,
    One refreshing, fair as thee.

Shrouding mists and gloomy shadows
    Vanish from her face away;
Strength restored to all the weary
    Is the promise of this day.

Into deeps no eye dared measure
    Dart its beams of heavenly light,
With new hope all fear dispelling
    Of death's dark and dreadful night.

NEW HOPE.

Life has pierced the tomb, arousing
   Joyful echoes; in the air
Spirits hover; hearts are glowing;
   Waking life is everywhere.

And where an abyss appalled us,
   Where was set our boundary stone,
Stands the risen One, extending
   Hands that wait to clasp our own.

Prince of life! 'mid morning's splendors,
   Come Thy messengers divine,
Bringing for both dead and living
   Peace-bestowing word of Thine!

Over all mankind the blessing
   Of that precious peace outpour;
Peace to every house; to every
   Grave be peace forevermore.

From the German.
S. C. R.

"OH, LIGHTLY PART, YE PURPLE CLOUDS."

OH, lightly part, ye purple clouds,
    Across the eastern skies!
Swing softly back, ye gates of gold,—
    Beyond whose portal lies
That mystic realm where days are born,—
And usher in the Easter morn!

The last pale star is lingering still,
    With wistful glance on high,
As fain to watch the sacred dawn
    Break o'er the bending sky,
And shed her latest, tenderest ray
In blessing on the new-born day.

'Tis Easter morn! No more the world
    Lies hushed in silent gloom;
No more the sepulchre's dread walls
    The living Lord entomb;

"OH, LIGHTLY PART."

Rejoice!—the stone is rolled away;
The Lord is risen,—'tis Easter day!

O Lilies! ope your fairest buds
    To greet this gracious morn;
And, Roses, in your crimson hearts
    Be sweetest odors born,
To rise and float upon the air,
Like sighs that saints have breathed in prayer.

Ye tuneful Birds, that soar and sing
    So near the gates of Heaven,
To-day let new, diviner strains
    Unto your song be given;
Sing joyfully, as far ye fly,—
"The Lord is risen, He reigns on high!"

O sorrowing Soul! that long hast kept
    Thy weary watch with sin,
Throw wide thy darkened doors to-day,
    And let the sunshine in:—
Be sad no more; lift up thine eye!
"The Lord is risen, He reigns on high!"

"OH, LIGHTLY PART."

The Lord is risen ! O Earth, rejoice !
    Thy myriad voices raise,
Till Heaven's blue arches ring again
    With songs of solemn praise ;
And far resounds th' exultant cry,—
'The Lord is risen, He reigns on high !"

MRS. LOUISE W. TILDEN.

THE MERRY CHURCH BELLS.

LET the merry church bells ring,
    Hence with tears and sighing;
Frost and cold are fled from spring,
    Love hath conquered dying.
Flowers are smiling, fields are gay,
    Sunny is the weather;
With our risen Lord to-day
    All things rise together.

Let the birds sing out again
    From their leafy chapel,
Praising Him with whom, in vain
    Satan sought to grapple.
Sounds of joy come fast and thick,
    As the breezes flutter—
"Resurrexit! non est hic!"
    Is the strain they utter.

THE MERRY CHURCH BELLS.

Let the thought of grief be past :
   This our comfort giveth—
He was slain on Friday last,
   But to-day He liveth.
Mourning heart must needs be gay,
   Nor let sorrow vex it :
Since the very grave can say,
   "Christus resurrexit!"

"HALLELUJAH, RAISE THE SONG.

HALLELUJAH, raise the song!
   "Jesus Christ is risen;"
Let the Church the note prolong,
   "Jesus Christ is risen!"
Her loving and triumphant Head,
Captivity has captive led,
And ev'ry foe has vanquishèd.
          Hallelujah!

Hallelujah! let the cry
   "Jesus Christ is risen,"
Wake each harp-string of the sky,
   "Jesus Christ is risen!"
The Sealèd Stone is rolled away,
Death and the grave have lost their prey,
For Jesus Christ is risen to-day.
          Hallelujah!

"HALLELUJAH, RAISE THE SONG."

Hallelujah ! dry the tear,
  " Jesus Christ is risen ; "
Sound o'er every silent bier,
  " Jesus Christ is risen ! "
Thrice blessèd pledge, ye mourners keep,
Who for your loved and lost ones weep,
Because He *lives*, they only sleep—
  Hallelujah !

Hallelujah ! let the sound,
  " Jesus Christ is risen,"
Circulate the world around,
  " Jesus Christ is risen ! "
Soon may the World's great Easter be,
When, her now bondaged children free,
Exultant, Lord, shall reign with Thee.
  Hallelujah !

J. R. MACDUFF.

A CAROL.

GOD hath sent His angels
    To the earth again,
Bringing joyful tidings
    To the sons of men ;
They who first at Christmas
    Thronged the heavenly way,
Now beside the tomb door
    Sit on Easter day.

CHORUS.

Angels, sing His triumph,
    As you sang His birth,
Christ the Lord is risen,
    " Peace, good-will on earth."

In the dreadful desert,
    Where the Lord was tried,
There the faithful angels
    Gathered at His side ;

A CAROL.

And, when in the garden,
 Grief, and pain, and care,
Bowed Him down with anguish,
 They were with Him there.
  Cho.—Angels, sing.

Yet the Christ they honor
 Is the same Christ still
Who, in light and darkness,
 Did His Father's will;
And the tomb deserted
 Shineth like the sky,
Since He passed out from it
 Into victory.
  Cho.—Angels, sing.

God has still His angels,
 Helping at His word
All His faithful children,
 Like their faithful Lord,
Soothing them in sorrow,
 Arming them in strife,

A CAROL.

Opening wide the tomb doors,
Leading into Life.
  Cho.—Angels, sing.

Father, send Thine angels
 Unto us, we pray;
Leave us not to wander;
 All along our way
Let them guard and guide us,
 Wheresoe'er we be,
Till our Resurrection
 Brings us home to Thee.
  Cho.—Angels, sing.

THE LORD IS RISEN INDEED!

THE Lord is risen indeed! Oh, hasten with
    the tidings;
He liveth who was dead—the Victor-King.
Death hath no more dominion: sing, oh! sing
    exulting;
Haste with this message to the sorrowing.

The Lord is risen indeed! The path of life
    He shows us;
  Sing, O ye heavens! and earth, responsive
    raise
Loud Alleluias, while on earth is dawning
  The Resurrection Morn, the Day of days.

The Lord is risen indeed! Oh, haste then to
    adore Him:
  Behold, 'tis He from out whose piercèd side

Was poured the life-blood that should be thy
    ransom :
    Behold, He liveth ! He who for thee died !

The Lord is risen indeed ! Rejoice ! for since
    He liveth,
    Ye too shall live who of His death partake ;
Partakers also of His resurrection,
    Ye in your Saviour's likeness shall awake.

The Lord is risen indeed ! Amen and Alle-
    luia !
    Where is thy victory, Grave ? where, Death,
        thy sting ?
The Lord is risen indeed ! Awake the peal-
    ing anthem !
    Around the circling earth let Alleluias ring !

Y. Y. K.

THE RESURRECTION LIGHT.

WHEN to the rock-hewn tomb they brought
    The lifeless Lord, with bitter tears,
And lingered, lost in sorrowing thought,
    And saw no end to doubts and fears;

When wondering at the works divine,
    And wondering at the shameful death,
And at the last attesting sign—
    Earth shaken by a dying breath;—

'Mid all these questionings and fears
    Did some sweet spirit whisper trust,—
That He who dried the widow's tears
    Would raise His own cold form from dust?

Ah, blessed grave! which friendship there
    Yielded to hold the sacred clay
That mutely claimed such pious care,
    The Crucified is here to-day.

THE RESURRECTION LIGHT.

He comes not asking for a tomb,—
   A sweeter boon may love supply;
The Lord is risen! He seeks a home,
   A human soul to occupy.

Far holier than the hallowed place
   Where once in death the Saviour lay,
Is every heart made pure by grace
   To entertain the Lord to-day.

What need to seek Him 'midst the dead?
   Behold! within the sacred walls
With us He sits, and breaks the bread;
   On us His benediction falls;—

" Peace!" Let Thy peace, O Friend divine,
   Abide with us by day, by night,
Till the eternal morning shine
   From Thee, the Resurrection Light.

                        E. D. R.

"OUT OF THE DUST AND THE DARKNESS."

OUT of the dust and the darkness,
    Up from the gloom and the cold,
Bourgeon the lilies of Easter,
    Lamps with a taper of gold;
Whiter than snow in the sunlight,
    Purer than altar-fed flame,
They bloom round the feet of the Master,
    And shine to the praise of His name.

Weak were our hearts when they laid Him
    Away in the tomb of the rock,
Veiled were our faces in sorrow—
    The Shepherd was gone from the flock.
Low bent the sad sky o'er the prison
    That earth, without Jesus, became:
Alleluia! The Lord hath arisen,
    Be glory and thanks to His name.

"OUT OF THE DUST."

Three days did the grave-silence hold Him,
   Three days was He hidden from sight,
While the scorner was proud in his scorning,
   And the faithless was lost in the night.
Three days! but all heaven for joyance!
   While the hosts of the ransomed proclaim
The grace of the love that redeemed them,
   And gathered them home in His name.

Sweet lilies of Easter, ye chide us,
   That still for our cherished ones gone,
We weep in the shadow of midnight,
   And not in the break of the dawn.
Our passionate pleading and yearning,
   The hope of the exile would shame;
For we know not our Lord in the garden,
   Nor turn though He calleth by name.

In the light of the Lord's resurrection
   His people should conquerors be;
In the battle with evil triumphant,
   From the terror of death ever free,

"OUT OF THE DUST."

We shall sleep in the dust and the darkness;
  We shall waken and sing to His name
Who will bring us to life everlasting
  By the path that, a victor, He came.

MARGARET E. SANGSTER.

"WHEN DAWNS ON EARTH THE EASTER SUN."

WHEN dawns on earth the Easter sun,
    The dear saints feel an answering thrill,
With whitest flowers their hands they fill,
And singing all in unison,

Unto the battlements they press,—
    The very marge of heaven—how near!
    And bend and look upon us here,
With eyes that rain down tenderness.

Their roses, brimmed with fragrant dew,
    Their lilies fair, they raise on high;
    "Rejoice! The Lord is risen!" they cry;
"Christ is arisen, we prove it true!

" Rejoice, and dry those faithless tears
    With which your Easter flowers are stained;

Share in our bliss, who have attained
The rapture of the eternal years.

"How proud the promise which endures,
　The Son that deigned, the Son that died;
　Have reached our haven by His side—
Are Christ's, but none the less are yours:

"Yours with a nearness never known
　While parted by the veils of sense;
　Infinite knowledge, joy intense,
A love which is not love alone,

"But faith perfected, vision free,
　And patience limitless and wise—
　Beloved, the Lord is risen, arise!
And dare to be as glad as we!"

We do rejoice, we do give thanks,
　Oh! blessed ones, for all you gain,
　As dimly through these mists of pain
We catch the gleaming of your ranks.

"WHEN DAWNS ON EARTH."

We will arise, with zeal increased,
   Blending the while we strive and grope,
   Our palm festival of Hope,
With your fruition's perfect feast.

Bend low, beloved; against the blue;
   Lift higher still the lilies fair,
   Till, following where our treasures are,
We come to join the feast with you.

SUSAN COOLIDGE.

AT THE SEPULCHRE.

A LITTLE band of weeping women went
    At early dawn to seek the sepulchre
Where Jesus had been laid. Sweet spices, myrrh
And precious ointments bringing, all intent
    On loving service. And thus walking, they
    Fell wondering who should roll the stone away;
When lo, they find the door is open wide—
But where is He who had been crucified?
    The grave-clothes folded lie, and in His stead
Two angels sit, with faces like the light,
    And say, "Why seek the quick among the dead?
    He is not here, but risen, as He had said."

Then, while they trembling stood, still nea came
The loving Mary Magdalene, the same

Whose many sins had been forgiven her.
She, finding not the Lord within the sepul-
    chre,
Fell weeping in her sorrow and affright,
Nor deemed the angels could have told her
    right.
When lo, a voice falls on her startled ear,
Whose accents she no more had hoped to
    hear.
With sorrow's flood still flowing down her
    cheek
She turns to hear her Lord and Master speak.

When weeping o'er some sepulchre of clay
    That held the one unto our souls most dear,
So to our questioning hearts the angels say,
    "He whom ye seek, beloved, is not here;
Lo, he is risen, but a little way
He goeth before. Be comforted and pray."

M. K. BUCK.

SWEET SURPRISES.

THEY sought Thy tomb, Thou Saviour sweet,
  Those early seekers true and sad;
But Thou their Living Lord didst meet
  And make Thy mourning lovers glad.

The friends as on their way they went,
  With troubled faces, talked of Thee;
When Thou didst suddenly present
  Thy comfort and Thy company.

They met in fear, they met by night,
  Those shrinking servants, Lord, of Thine;
When sudden shone Thy presence bright,
  And sounded sweet Thy voice divine.

Thou who thus sweetly didst surprise,
  Dost Thou not still Thy seekers bless?

SWEET SURPRISES.

And still to loving, weeping eyes,
   Appear in sudden gloriousness?

Dost Thou not in their sorest need
   Thy fainting servants still renew?
And still their dearest hope exceed,
   And still their best desire outdo?

To us Thy tremblers, Lord, appear,
   With us Thy weary pilgrims walk!
Delight our banquets with Thy cheer,
   And lift to heights divine our talk!

On us in sudden brightness break,
   For us repeat each sweet surprise;
Our hearts will burn when Thou dost speak,
   Our earth-bound souls with Thee will rise.

                                   THOMAS H. GILL.

"THIS SAME JESUS."

" And a sign shall be granted to the doubt of love which is denied to the doubt of indifference."

THE Magdalen stood weeping in the garden,
    That early Sunday morning long ago ;
The sky that bent above was pale with twilight,
    The far-off East blushed with a crimson glow.

Her loving heart was sore almost to breaking,
    No sadder tears than hers were ever shed ;
Her hope had faded out in utter darkness,
    The Lord she loved and trusted so, *was dead*.

Yes, He was dead—the Shiloh, the Anointed !
    She saw the cross, she heard the last great cry,
And all was over now. They had mistaken
    His rank and mission ; oh ! that she might die !

And yet, who ever was so kind and gentle?
  Disease and death before His touch had fled,
And she herself had felt that power of healing;
  He was her Master, though He lay there dead.

We know the rest; we know how Jesus found her,
  As she stood sadly by the tomb alone,
And spoke her name in tones so sweet and tender
  She knew the loving voice must be His own.

We have no need to stand and weep with Mary,
  For He who rose that day shall weep no more;
Yet sometimes now, our eyes grow dim with sorrow,
  We can not see the Lord whom we adore,

And gloomy doubts rise up like clouds before us;
  " Is what we counted gain an utter loss ?

"THIS SAME JESUS."

Is it a dream, a myth, the blessed story
   Of Christ our Saviour and His precious
      cross?"

O friends! bring not your spices to embalm
      Him,
   The Lord you seek is risen from the grave;
He knows the feeble faith, the sore tempta-
      tions,
   Of those that once He gave His life to save.

The highest blessing waits for the believing,
   But Christ the Lord has gifts for all His own;
Of old, to one who, doubting Him, yet loved
      Him,
   The nail-prints in His hands and feet were
      shown.

"Give us a sign!" cries out the world that
      hates Him,
   The Master, as of old, makes no reply;
But, to the heart of every true disciple,
   Be sure the blessed Saviour will draw nigh,

"THIS SAME JESUS."

And call each one by name, as He did Mary;
   And, though the stone seemed rolled before
      the door,
The risen Lord Himself shall stand before you,
   For Jesus is the same forevermore.

N. Y. Observer.

"O COMFORT YE MY PEOPLE!"

"O COMFORT ye my people!"
   All sadness put away;
The bells from many a steeple
   Ring in the Easter Day!
Unto the grave with weeping
   They came, that morn of gloom,
And angels watch were keeping
   Within the open tomb.

For when the day was breaking,
   And ere the shadows fled,
Our King, His glory taking,
   Had risen from the dead.
Finished redemption's story,
   And from the waiting throng
Of angel hosts in glory,
   Rang out the glad new song.

"O COMFORT YE MY PEOPLE."

Victor, and King immortal
   Entering the lifted gates,
Open He left the portal,
   And there in love He waits.
To-day with glad confessing
   Angels and saints on high,
Sing honor, praise, and blessing
   To Him who came to die.

To-day the lilies springing
   From Winter's gloom and cold,
Sweet bells of Easter, ringing,
   Tell the glad song of old—
That Christ indeed is risen,
   And all His saints shall rise,
Fair flowers from death's cold prison,
   To bloom in Paradise.

Shall these eyes, too, behold Thee,
   O King, in all Thy grace?
That far-off land, 'tis told me,
   Gives sinful souls a place.

"O COMFORT YE MY PEOPLE."

    Rejoice, O soul, in gladness,
        To-day thou'rt newly born ;
    To banish all thy sadness
        Christ rose this Easter morn.

M. R. J.

EASTER LESSONS.

I.

OUR summers are but burial-places, where
    We lay to rest the sweet days as they die,
Softening their outlines with love's rosemary,
And memory's lavender, and all of rare
          Tokens to keep them fair.

II.

Our winters are the vaults, whose ice-fring'd
    cells
    Shut in our sorrow-shrouded days, for whom
    When borne and left amid their frozen gloom,
White-surpliced flakes, in place of lily-bells,
          Tinkle their muffled knells.

III.

We bury them, and sigh with bowing head,
    Submissive else. The tender days *must* go,

For they are earthly-born, and perish so ;
Yet by what augury hath any said
         That they are wholly dead ?

IV.

The short, child-meted grave o'er which we
   yearn
  Even yet—the empty bird's-nest filled with
   snows—
  The leafless bough—the Spring that comes
   and goes,
Teach resurrection-lessons each in turn,
         Which we are quick to learn.

V.

Our days die thus ; and we, their lives with-
   drawn,
  Like other mourners, fail of faith's control,
  Forgetful that each memory is the soul
Of a dead day, such as in summers gone
         'Midst rosemary sleeps on.

VI.

And when they meet us yonder, face to face,
   In the grand Easter Morning, shall we then
   Hail them with greet and welcome once again,
Companions of our blessedness always,
       Dear, risen, deathless days?

MARGARET J. PRESTON.

AN EASTER SONG.

OUT of dust and darkness comes a cry of
    passion;
Out of loss and sorrow wakes a sudden thrill;
Sick we are and weary of life's hollow fashion,
    Hear us, Lord, and answer, dost Thou
    slumber still?

Heavy fall the shadows on the dim horizon,
    Veiled the stony eyes from wistful eyes be-
    low;
Cold and still Thou liest in Thine earthly
    prison;
    Whither, Lord and Master, whither shall
    we go?

Surely we have trusted—turned in faith and
    meekness
    To the arms extended and the thorn-crowned
    brow;

But, alas! Thou knowest all our human weakness,
   Faint we are and fearful—wilt Thou leave us now?

Harder weighs the burden on Thy toiling creatures,
   Faster crowd the evils Thou alone canst cure;
Through the time-mists dimmer shine Thy gracious features,
   Ah! the need is greater, is the hope as sure?

Fainting by the wayside, lo, we turn and listen;
   Through our tent of longing lift we weary eyes:
Will the Easter dawning once more gleam and glisten?
   Will the Christ we wait for yet once more arise?

AN EASTER SONG.

Lo, the strange, new Voices! lo, the scoffer's
    whisper:
  "He in whom you trusted passeth like the
    rest:
Sigh of aged mourner, breath of infant lisper—
    Naught shall stir an echo in that silent
    breast!"

Lord, the peril presses! Lord, the night-rack
    deeper
    Gathers o'er the pathway, rough for mortal
    feet;
Holds the sealèd gravestone still its pallid
    sleeper?
    Is the tale of human sorrows incomplete?

Peace! the deep gloom brightens! see, through
    yon dim distance
  Gleams a glow of glory, wakes a sudden ray!
Lo, the gracious guerdon of Faith's sweet per-
    sistence!
    Lo, the gentle dawning of Love's Easter
    Day!

AN EASTER SONG.

Hark! the anthem answers; listen! fast and
    faster
  Swells a psalm whose chorus angels shout
    abroad:
"Come, O Lord undying! Hail, O mighty
    Master!
  Lo, the risen Saviour! lo, the Christ of
    God!"

BARTON GREY.

THE DEAR OLD STORY.

O, THE winter of the world
    Was long and dreary :
The shadows stretched away
    And hearts were weary ;
At last the Sun of Love
    Burst forth in glory,
And this new Easter-tide
    Tells the old story.

Ye gold and purple blooms
    That greet the morning,
Earth gives you for a crown,
    Love's brow adorning.
O, everywhere the world
    Is starred with glory,
And in sweet flowery script
    Tells the old story.

THE DEAR OLD STORY.

Sad watchers at the tomb
    Hear the glad voices—
Look up, He is not there,
    The world rejoices.
Life hidden for a time
    Comes forth in glory—
All hail with songs of joy
    The dear old story.

M. F. BUTTS.

WOMAN'S EASTER.

WITH Mary, ere dawn, in the garden,
    I stand at the tomb of the Lord;
I share in her sorrowing wonder:
    I hear through the darkness a word,
The first the dear Master hath spoken
Since the awful death-stillness was broken.

He calleth her tenderly, "Mary!"
    Sweet, sweet is His voice in the gloom.
He spake to us first, O my sisters,
    So breathing our lives into bloom!
He lifteth our souls out of prison!
We earliest saw Him arisen.

He lives! Read you not the glad tidings
    In our eyes, that have gazed into His?
He lives! By His light on our faces
    Believe it, and come where He is!

O doubter, and you who denied Him,
Return to your places beside Him.

The message of His resurrection,
  To man, it was woman's to give :
It is fresh in her heart through the ages :—
  "He lives that you also may live.
Unfolding, as He hath, the story
Of manhood's attainable glory."

O Sun on our souls first arisen,
  Give us light for the spirits that grope;
Make us loving and steadfast and loyal,
  To bear up humanity's hope ;
O Friend who forsakest us never,
Breathe through us Thy errands forever.

LUCY LARCOM.

THE CROCUS CROSS.

WHEN light the purple crocus springs,
    And lifts to heaven its shining head,
My spirit on the morning's wings
    Seeks the far city of the dead,
Where kindred blossoms rise, I know,
Over the sleeping dust below.

I mind me of the winter day,
    The sunny sky, the grave new made,
The Cross traced on the yielding clay,
    The tear-wet bulbs within it laid;
Dark and unlovely to our eyes,
Not like the beauty that should rise.

Safe planted from the storm and cold,
    We left them waiting for the hour
When wintry days should all be told,
    And spring awake the perfect flower:
The glorious form that should appear
From the dull roots we buried there.

THE CROCUS CROSS.

Not for the careless eye to see,
   The mystic cryptogram was set :
A mute appeal, our God, to Thee,
   A prayer that Thou would not forget,
Beneath that shadowed cross there lies
Somewhat of Thine that must arise.

And hast not Thou, with loving thought,
   Even in these flowers set Thy sign,
That so our grieving hearts be taught
   Thy resurrection's truth divine,
Each spring repeating to our eyes,
Thy word of comfort, " He shall rise ? "

Then let us rest in simple faith,
   On the sure promise Thou hast given :
We know that Thou hast conquered death,
   We know Thou rulest earth and heaven.
Fixed on Thy truth our hopes remain,
We know that " He shall rise again ! "

ANONYMOUS.

"EASTER LILIES, SWEET AND WHITE."

EASTER lilies, sweet and white,
    Full of beauty and of light,
Fill the Saviour's open tomb
With your glory and perfume—
Answering in your own calm way
What He said of you one day,
When upon the mountain's side
He rebuked our human pride,
Told us how our Father's care
Calls His anxious child to prayer,
Fearless faith and loving trust
In Him who raised you from the dust.

Ring, snow-white bells, your purest praise,
To glorify these Easter days,
    And let our risen Saviour's joy
    Your voiceless, fragrant breath employ—

"EASTER LILIES."

Fill every valley with perfume
And lighten death's appalling gloom.
Teach ye our troubled hearts the way
To trust our Saviour every day,
Until we see Him as He is,
And follow Him in endless bliss,
Who is alive and once was dead,
Our Risen and Triumphant Head.

Sweet valley lilies! braving now
The north wind's blast, the latter snow,
Heralds of spring and summer time,
Your odors shed through every clime,
And celebrate His wondrous fame
Who called Himself by your sweet name,
And left the world this emblem dear,
Of perfect love which casts out fear.

W. J. R. TAYLOR.

THE EASTER GUEST.

I KNEW Thou wert coming, O Lord Divine!
   I felt in the sunlight a softened shine;
A murmur of welcome I thought I heard
In the ripple of brook and the chirp of bird;
And the bursting buds and the springing grass
Seemed to be waiting to see Thee pass;
And the sky and the sea and the throbbing sod
Pulsed and thrilled at the touch of God!

I knew Thou wert coming, O Love Divine!
To gather the world's heart up in Thine.
I knew the bonds of the rock-hewn grave
Were riven, that, living, Thy life might save;
But, blind and wayward, I could not see
Thou wert coming to dwell with *me*, e'en *me*,
And my heart, o'erburdened with care and sin,
Had no fair chambers to take Thee in.

THE EASTER GUEST.

Not one clean spot for Thy foot to tread,
Not one pure pillow to rest Thy head.
There was nothing to offer—no bread, no wine,
No oil of joy in this heart of mine;
And yet the light of Thy Kingly face
Illumed for Thyself one small, dark place,
And I crept to the spot, by Thy smile made sweet,
And my tears sprang, ready to wash Thy feet.

Now let me come nearer, O Christ Divine!
Make in my soul for Thyself a shrine;
Cleanse, till the desolate place shall be
Fit for a dwelling, dear Lord, for Thee!
Rear, if Thou wilt, a throne in my breast;
Reign! I will worship and serve my Guest.
Abide Thou in me, if in Thee I abide.
What end shall there be to the Easter-tide?

MARY LOWE DICKINSON.

GOD'S FLOWERS UPON GOD'S ALTAR.

'TIS "of Thine own we give Thee," gracious God !
Flowers of the spring-time, offerings from the sod,
Tinted by Thine own hand with rainbow dyes,
Or with the gold and blue of sunset skies.
Of all earth's boundless gifts, to Thee we bring
Nought that is holier as an offering.

Oh ! glorious symbols of the Easter morn,
Out of decay and death and darkness born,
Springing to light and life from out the tomb
Of nature's desolation, sadness, gloom :
Ye come, sweet flowers, with fragrance pure and rare,
To blend your incense with the breath of prayer.

Christ hath arisen " with healing in His wings."
Ye have arisen, oh, bright and beauteous
   things,
To tell us of that resurrection morn,
When we, immortal, from the grave new-born,
With bodies glorified, to life shall rise,
And meet the Saviour in the bending skies!

ESTHER W. BARNES.

"WAKE, MY CHILDREN!"

WAKE, my children, it is Easter!
    See the bright sky overhead,
See the joyous sunbeams dancing:
    Christ is risen from the dead!

Waken, children! early greet Him,
    On this happy, blessed morn,
Far more happy, far more blessed,
    Than the day our Lord was born.

Greet Him with your first Good-morning,
    With your earliest smiles Him greet;
Loving words and sunny tempers
    Are to Him like spices sweet.

Early hasten to His temple,
    Fragrant with its Easter flowers;

"WAKE, MY CHILDREN."

Give Him, then, your heart's best worship,
  Morning's fresh and lovely hours.

Of your lives be this the emblem :
  Seek Him in the morn of youth ;
Choose Him for your Heavenly Leader,
  Who will guide you to all Truth.

ANONYMOUS.

"SING, CHILDREN, SING!"

SING, children, sing!
    And the lily censers swing,
Sing that life and joy are waking and that
    Death no more is king;
Sing the happy, happy tumult of the slowly
    brightening Spring!
    Sing, little children, sing!

    Sing, children, sing!
    Winter wild has taken wing,
Fill the air with the sweet tidings till the frosty
    echoes ring!
Along the eaves the icicles no longer glitter-
    ing cling;
And the crocus in the garden lifts its bright
    face to the sun,
And in the meadows softly the brooks begin
    to run,

"SING, CHILDREN, SING!"

And the golden catkins swing
In the warm airs of the Spring ;
   Sing, little children, sing !

   Sing, children, sing !
   The lilies white you bring
In the joyous Easter morning for hope are
   blossoming ;
And as the earth her shroud of snow from off
   her breast doth fling,
So may we cast our fetters off in God's eternal
   Spring.
So may we find release at last from sorrow
   and from pain,
So may we find our childhood's calm, delicious
   dawn again.

Sweet are your eyes, oh, little ones, that look
   with smiling grace,
Without a shade of doubt or fear into the
   Future's face !

"SING, CHILDREN, SING!"

Sing, sing in happy chorus, with joyful voices tell
That death is life and God is good, and all things shall be well;
That bitter days shall cease
In warmth and light and peace—
That Winter yields to Spring—
    Sing, little children, sing!

CELIA THAXTER.

AN EASTER PRAYER.

OH, let me know
    The power of Thy resurrection ;
      Oh, let me show
Thy risen life in calm and clear reflection ;
      Oh, let me soar
Where Thou, my Saviour Christ, art gone
    before ;
      In mind and heart
Let me dwell always, only, where Thou art.

      Oh, let me give
Out of the gifts Thou freely givest ;
      Oh, let me live
With life abundantly because Thou livest ;
      Oh, make me shine
In darkest places, for Thy light is mine ;
      Oh, let me be
A faithful witness for Thy truth and Thee.

AN EASTER PRAYER.

      Oh, let me show
The strong reality of gospel story;
      Oh, let me go
From strength to strength, from glory unto
    glory;
      Oh, let me sing
For very joy, because Thou art my King;
      Oh, let me praise
Thy love and faithfulness through all my days.

                FRANCES RIDLEY HAVERGAL.

MYRRH-BEARERS.

(*The First Easter Morning*).

THREE women crept at break of day
    Agrope along the shadowy way
Where Joseph's tomb and garden lay.

With blanch of woe each face was white,
As the grey Orient's waxing light
Brought back upon their awe-struck sight

The sixth day scene of anguish : Fast
The starkly-standing cross they passed,
And breathless neared the gate at last.

Each on her throbbing bosom bore
A burden of such fragrant store
As never there had lain before.

MYRRH-BEARERS.

Spices the purest, richest, best,
That e'er the musky East possessed,
From Ind to Araby-the-Blest,

Had they with sorrow-riven hearts
Searched all Jerusalem's costliest marts
In quest of — nards whose pungent arts

Should the dead sepulchre imbue
With vital odors through and through :—
'Twas all their love had leave to do !

The risen Christ was gone !   And yet
Did either Mary once regret
Her offering ?   Did Salomé fret

Over the unused aloes ?   Nay !
They counted not, that Easter-Day,
As waste, what they had brought : the way

Home seemed the path to heaven.   They bare
Thenceforth, about the robes they wear,
The clinging perfume everywhere.

* * * * * *

Myrrh-Bearers still—at home, abroad,
What paths have holy women trod
Burdened with votive gifts for God—

Rare gifts, whose chiefest worth was priced
By this one thought that all sufficed ;—
Their spices had been bruised for Christ!

MARGARET J. PRESTON.

EASTER SUNDAY.

NOT ours to breathe that early air,
    Not ours that fragrant store to bring,
And at the open sepulchre
    To find the Angel's radiant wing.

Not ours sad Mary's tears to weep
    O'er the stolen treasures of that grave ;
Not ours that mournful watch to keep—
    Not ours that vanished form to crave.

Not for our eyes the Vision bright
    Of that dear form beheld once more ;
Those tones our ears may not delight,
    Nor hands of ours those wounds explore.

Yet shineth full on our glad eyes
    The lustre of that wondrous morn ;
For as the Lord of life doth rise ;
    Our Lord, our Master is new-born.

EASTER SUNDAY.

Yes, ours the gain without the loss!
    The glory ours without the gloom!
Naught but our refuge-place the Cross,
    Naught but our treasure-house that Tomb.

The grief that streamed from Mary's eyes,
    On settled spirits may not move;
Yet with her joy our gladness vies
    To greet the Master whom we love.

We meet no fearful throng by night,
    We dread no tidings dolorous;
Yet shines 'midst us the Saviour bright,
    Yet speaketh He sweet peace to us.

No lips of ours the news gainsay,
    No witness do our hands require;
O sure and sweet the hold we lay
    Upon the Lord of our desire.

We envy not the eyes that saw,
    Since God hath given our eyes to see;

EASTER SUNDAY.

O souls thrice blessèd, that could draw
   Thy latest blessing, Lord, from Thee!

We sweetly store those words divine,
   And lowly wait and trustful love,
Till bright on us Thy face shall shine,
   And ours shall be Thy smile above.

THOMAS H. GILL.

THE EASTER GREETING.

WHY weepest thou?—to Mary Magdalen
    Came the first joy of resurrection
  greeting:
Still, through the gloom of tears and grief,
    again
  We hear that voice, the Easter words repeat-
    ing;
        Why weepest thou?

Why weepest thou?—unknown, yet still the
    same,
  The Heavenly Gardener, bearing flowers
    immortal,
Beside thee stands, to call thee by thy name,
  And point to Eden's ever-open portal:—
        Why weepest thou?

THE EASTER GREETING.

Why weepest thou?—is the departed Lord
  By wrong and judgment from thy presence
    taken?
Look up—behold Him! by the grave restored,
  In Godlike power from death's short night
    to waken;—
      Why weepest thou?

Why weepest thou?—is there a load of sin
  That seals the sepulchre with weight oppress-
    ing?
Only thy dead transgression lies within;
  Without thy Lord draws near with par-
    d'ning blessing;—
      Why weepest thou?

Why weepest thou?—is it that earthly care
  Darkens thy life with tempest clouds of
    sorrow?
Look up, behold, in Heaven how pure and fair,
  Dawns on the night of death the Easter
    morrow;—
      Why weepest thou?

THE EASTER GREETING.

Why weepest thou?—over the long-mourn'd dead?
Only the mortal part with earth is blended,
Far from the tomb, in paths where Jesus led,
   Homeward the spirit has to God ascended;
      Why weepest thou?

Why weepest thou?—in the long journey's gloom
   Do the slow years delay thy heav'nward yearning?
Lo! He awaits thee in the Father's Home,
   There worn feet rest, from pilgrim toil returning;—
      Why weepest thou?

Why weepest thou?—Lord, Thou hast given each day
Some drops of joy in every cup of sadness;
Soon Thou wilt wipe all tears of grief away,
   There, where Heaven's songs repeat the words of gladness,
      Why weepest thou?

From the German, by
AUGUSTA C. HAYWARD.

HE IS THY LIFE.

I.
JESUS, Thy life is mine !
   Dwell evermore in me ;
    And let me see
That nothing can untwine
    My life from Thine.

II.
Thy life in me be shown !
   Lord, I would henceforth seek
    To think and speak
Thy thoughts, Thy words alone,
    No more my own.

III.
Thy love, Thy joy, Thy peace,
   Continuously impart
    Unto my heart ;
Fresh springs, that never cease,
    But still increase.

HE IS THY LIFE.

IV.

The blest reality
  Of resurrection power,
    Thy Church's dower,
Life more abundantly,
    Lord, give to me!

V.

Thy fullest gift, O Lord,
  Now at Thy feet I claim,
    Through Thy dear name!
And touch the rapturous chord
  Of praise forth poured.

VI.

Jesus, my life is Thine,
  And evermore shall be
    Hidden in Thee!
For nothing can untwine
  Thy life from mine.

FRANCES RIDLEY HAVERGAL.

THE INESTIMABLE LOVE.

"We bless Thee for our creation, preservation, and all the blessings of this life; but above all, for Thine inestimable love in the redemption of the world by our Lord Jesus Christ."
HANDEL'S Messiah.

HUSH! for a master harp is tuned again,
   In truest unison with choirs above,
For prelude to a loftier, sweeter strain,
   The praise of God's inestimable love;
Who sent redemption to a world of woe,
That all a Father's heart His banished ones might know.

Hush! while on silvery wing of holiest song
   Floats forth the old, dear story of our peace,
His coming, the Desire of Ages long,
   To wear our chains, and win our glad release.
Our wondering joy, to hear such tidings blest,
Is crowned with "Come to Him, and He will give you rest."

THE INESTIMABLE LOVE.

Rest, by His sorrow! Bruisèd for our sin,
    Behold the Lamb of God! His death our
        life.
Now lift your heads, ye gates! He entereth in,
    Christ risen indeed, and Conqueror in the
        strife.
Thanks, thanks to Him who won, and Him
        who gave
Such victory of love, such triumph o'er the
        grave.

Hark! "Hallelujah!" Oh, sublimest strain!
    Is it prophetic echo of the day
When He, our Saviour and our King, shall
        reign,
    And all the earth shall own His righteous
        sway?
Lift heart and voice, and swell the mighty
        chords,
While hallelujahs peal, to Him, the Lord of
        lords!

THE INESTIMABLE LOVE.

" Worthy of all adoration
   Is the Lamb that once was slain,"
Cry, in raptured exultation,
His redeemed from every nation ;
   Angel myriads join the strain,
Sounding from their sinless strings
Glory to the King of kings :
Harping with their harps of gold,
Praise which never can be told.

Hallelujahs full and swelling
   Rise around His throne of might.
All our highest laud excelling,
Holy and Immortal, dwelling
   In the unapproachèd light ;
He is worthy to receive
All that heaven and earth can give,
Blessing, honor, glory, might,
All are His by glorious right.

As the sound of many waters
   Let the full Amen arise !

THE INESTIMABLE LOVE.

Hallelujah ! Ceasing never
Sounding through the great forever,
   Linking all its harmonies ;
Through eternities of bliss,
Lord, our rapture shall be this,
And our endless life shall be
One Amen of praise to Thee !

FRANCES RIDLEY HAVERGAL.

FOREVER WITH THE LORD!

O SWEET home-echo on the pilgrim's way!
  Thrice welcome message from a land of light!
As through a clouded sky the moonbeams stray,
  So on Eternity's deep shrouded night
Streams a mild radiance, from that cheering word,
"So shall we be forever with the Lord!"

At home with Jesus! He who went before
  For His own people mansions to prepare;
The soul's deep longings filled, its conflicts o'er,
  All rest and blessedness with Jesus there;—
What home like this can the wide earth afford?
"So shall we be forever with the Lord!"

FOREVER WITH THE LORD.

With Him all gathered! to that blessed home,
   Through all its windings still the pathway
      tends,
While ever and anon bright glimpses come
   Of that fair City where the journey ends :
Where all of bliss is centred in one word,—
" So shall we be forever with the Lord."

Here, kindred hearts are severed far and wide,
   By many a weary mile of land and sea,
Or life's all-varied cares and paths divide—
   But yet a joyful gathering shall be ;
The broken links repaired, the lost restored,
"So shall we be forever with the Lord."

And is there ever perfect union here ?
   Ah! daily sins, lamented and confest,
They come between us and the friends most
      dear,
   They mar our blessedness and break our
      rest.

FOREVER WITH THE LORD.

With life we leave the evils long deplored,—
" So shall we be forever with the Lord."

All prone to error—none set wholly free
   From the old serpent's soul-ensnaring chain,
The truths one child of God can clearly see,
   He seeks to make his brother feel in vain;
But all shall harmonize in heaven's full chord,
" So shall we be forever with the Lord."

O precious promise, mercifully given,
   Well may it soothe the wail of earthly woe;
O'er the dark passage to the gates of heaven
   The light of hope and resurrection throw!
Thanks for the blessed, life-inspiring word,
" So shall we be forever with the Lord!"

From the German.
H. L. L.

Agnus Dei, we are guilty;
   Panis Vitæ, we are faint;
But Thou didst not rise at Easter,
   To be deaf to our complaint.
Come, oh come, to cleanse and feed us,
   Breathing peace and kindling love,
Till Thy Paschal blessings bear us
   To the Feast of feasts above.
W. B.

www.ingramcontent.com/pod-product-compliance
Lightning Source LLC
Chambersburg PA
CBHW032244080426
42735CB00008B/988